WORLD OF WONDER

INCREDIBLE RAIN FOREST

Written by Kay Barnham

Illustrated by Maddie Frost

CRABTREE
PUBLISHING COMPANY
WWW.CRABTREEBOOKS.COM

CRABTREE
PUBLISHING COMPANY
WWW.CRABTREEBOOKS.COM

Author: Kay Barnham

Editorial Director: Kathy Middleton

Editors: Victoria Brooker, Janine Deschenes

Proofreader: Melissa Boyce

Creative director: Paul Cherrill

Illustrator: Maddie Frost

Production coordinator and
Prepress technician: Tammy McGarr

Print coordinator: Katherine Berti

Words with lines underneath, like this, can be found in the glossary on page 32.

Library and Achives Canada Cataloguing in Publication

Title: Incredible rain forests / written by Kay Barnham ;
  illustrated by Maddie Frost.
Other titles: Incredible rainforests
Names: Barnham, Kay, author. | Frost, Maddie, illustrator.
Description: Series statement: World of wonder | Originally published under title:
  Incredible rainforests. London: Wayland, 2018. |
  Includes bibliographical references and index.
Identifiers: Canadiana (print) 20200220373 | Canadiana (ebook) 20200220381
  ISBN 9780778782483 (hardcover) |
  ISBN 9780778782520 (softcover) | ISBN 9781427126214 (HTML)
Subjects: LCSH: Rain forests—Juvenile literature. |
  LCSH: Rain forest ecology—Juvenile literature.
Classification: LCC QH86 .B37 2021 | DDC j577.34—dc23

Library of Congress Cataloging-in-Publication Data

Names: Barnham, Kay, author. | Frost, Maddie, illustrator.
Title: Incredible rain forests / written by Kay Barnham ;
  illustrated by Maddie Frost.
Description: New York : Crabtree Publishing Company, 2021. |
  Series: World of wonder | First published in 2018 by Wayland.
Identifiers: LCCN 2020015586 (print) | LCCN 2020015587 (ebook) |
  ISBN 9780778782483 (hardcover) |
  ISBN 9780778782520 (paperback) | ISBN 9781427126214 (ebook)
Subjects: LCSH: Rain forests--Juvenile literature.
Classification: LCC QH86 .B369 2021 (print) | LCC QH86 (ebook) |
  DDC 577.34--dc23
LC record available at https://lccn.loc.gov/2020015586
LC ebook record available at https://lccn.loc.gov/2020015587

Crabtree Publishing Company

www.crabtreebooks.com   1-800-387-7650
Published by Crabtree Publishing Company in 2021

First published in 2018 by Wayland
Copyright ©Hodder and Stoughton 2018

Printed in the U.S.A./072020/CG20200429

Published in Canada
Crabtree Publishing
616 Welland Avenue
St. Catharines, Ontario
L2M 5V6

Published in the United States
Crabtree Publishing
347 Fifth Ave
Suite 1402-145
New York, NY 10016

NOTES FOR PARENTS AND TEACHERS

This series encourages children to observe the wonderful world around them. Here are some ideas to help children get more out of this book.

 1 Make a rainforest collage on a piece of bristol board or cardboard. Use different materials such as fabric, photos, paint, and pieces of paper to create plants, trees, animals, and rivers.

 2 Ask children to write down as many rainforest animals as they can remember. Have them share their ideas and create a group list.

 3 Recycling helps the rain forests. How many things can children think of to recycle?

 4 Have a competition to build the tallest rainforest tree, using old newspapers. Then recycle them, of course!

Did you know that most <u>tropical rain forests</u> are near the equator? The equator is an imaginary line that runs around the middle of Earth.

The equator is closer to the Sun than any other
part of our planet. That means the weather
is very hot there. Rain forests have a lot of rain too.
There are different rain forests around the world.

A rain forest has giant trees
that reach toward the sky.
Below the tallest trees is
a roof of smaller treetops.
This is where most
animals live.

Shrubs and bushes grow in the shade
beneath the trees. At the bottom is the
forest floor, where few plants grow.

Plant leaves take in a gas called carbon dioxide.
Then they give out another gas called oxygen.
Humans and other living things breathe oxygen.

The hot, wet weather means that many plants grow well in rain forests. These plants create a lot of oxygen! This means that rain forests are important for all living creatures.

Each rain forest has its own <u>water cycle</u>.
The hot weather there causes the cycle
to happen quickly! First, <u>water vapor</u>
rises from the rain forest's plants.
Then clouds form above the rain forest.

When it rains, the thick forest roof catches many raindrops. Some rain gets to the forest floor. The plants take in the water. Then hot weather makes water vapor rise all over again.

Even though rain forests only
cover a small part of our planet,
they are home to many living things.

About two out of every three plant <u>species</u> grow in rain forests. Around half of all animal species live in rain forests too. People discover new species of plants and animals in rain forests all the time!

Plants need light to grow. In a rain forest, trees grow very tall so that the Sun can shine on them.

Vines are plants with long stems. Their stems climb up the trees to reach the sunlight at the top of a rain forest. Flowers such as orchids and many other plants grow among the high branches too.

There is a lot less sunlight at the forest floor.
The trees above block the light! The few plants
on the forest floor adapted to survive there.

Some rainforest plants use special chemicals
to scare away insects that try to eat them.
These chemicals can be very useful for humans too.
They can be used to make medicines!

Kingfishers, macaws, toucans, parrots, and hornbills
are colorful birds that live in rain forests.
They fly among the treetops.

The harpy eagle lives in rain forests too.
It is one of the largest birds of prey in the world.
A bird of prey is a bird that hunts and eats small animals.
The harpy eagle's wings measure
up to 6.5 feet (2 m) wide.

Monkeys, chimpanzees,
and orangutans leap among
rainforest trees. Meanwhile, sloths move
from branch to branch very slowly.

Below the trees, larger animals such as tigers, jaguars, leopards, and gorillas roam through different rain forests around the world.

So much rain falls that huge rivers often
run through rain forests. The Amazon River
flows through the Amazon rain forest.

The rivers are home to many animals. There are piranhas with sharp teeth and electric eels that give powerful shocks. Crocodiles, caimans, and anacondas lurk in the water too, hunting for their next meal.

Some of the trees in the Amazon rain forest
are more than one thousand years old!
But did you know that rain forests
have been on Earth for millions of years?

Scientists think that rain forests
may be even older than dinosaurs!

Every year, rainforest trees are cut down to make room for houses, mines, and farms. The wood from trees can be used as <u>fuel</u>. It can also be used to make paper, furniture, and homes.

When large areas of rainforest trees
are cut down, rainforest species
struggle to survive.

People know rainforest trees are very important.
They are trying to stop those who cut them down.
They are also planting new trees. We can help
by recycling and using less paper.

We must all work together
to save rain forests and the
plants and animals that live there!

THINGS TO DO

1. Paint your own rain forest, hiding as many rainforest animals as you can among the trees.

2. Many species in the rain forest are yet to be discovered, so invent your own animal. Go wild! Make it as colorful and amazing as you can!

3. Make a word cloud about the rain forest. Start with "RAIN FOREST" and then add any other words you can think of. Write them all down using different–colored pens. Start like this...

RAIN FOREST
TREES
VINES

LEARNING MORE

Books

Delano, Marfe Ferguson. *Rain Forests.* National Geographic Kids, 2017.

Kopp, Megan. *What Do You Find in a Rainforest Tree?* Crabtree Publishing, 2016.

Powell, Jillian. *Discover Through Craft: Rainforests.* Franklin Watts, 2017.

Websites

Enjoy these awesome rainforest games and activities.
www.rainforest-alliance.org/kids

Learn more about rain forests by reading new facts, checking out cool photos, and watching an interesting video.
www.kids.nationalgeographic. com/explore/nature/habitats/ rain-forest/

GLOSSARY

adapted Changed to better suit an environment

caimans Reptiles that look like alligators, found in Central and South America

fuel A material burned to make energy

gas A type of matter, such as air, that has no shape and expands freely

species Groups of living things that have common characteristics

survive To stay alive

tropical rain forests Forests with high amounts of rainfall per year and high temperatures, found near the equator

water cycle The ongoing way that water warms and rises into the atmosphere as water vapor, cools into clouds, and falls back to the ground as rain

water vapor Water that becomes a gas